Using Energy to Get Around

Andrew Einspruch

Smart Apple Media
P.O. Box 3263
Mankato, MN, 56002

First published in 2010 by
MACMILLAN EDUCATION AUSTRALIA PTY LTD
15–19 Claremont St, South Yarra, Australia 3141

Visit our web site at www.macmillan.com.au or go directly to www.macmillanlibrary.com.au

Associated companies and representatives throughout the world.

Copyright © Andrew Einspruch 2010

Library of Congress Cataloging-in-Publication Data

Einspruch, Andrew.
    Using energy to get around / Andrew Einspruch.
        p. cm. — (Living sustainably)
    Includes index.
    ISBN 978-1-59920-557-1 (library binding)
    1. Transportation—Energy conservation—Juvenile literature. 2. Sustainable living—Juvenile literature. I. Title.
    TJ163.5.T7E375 2011
    333.79'68—dc22
                                2009045103

Publisher: Carmel Heron   Designer: Kerri Wilson (cover and text)
Managing Editor: Vanessa Lanaway   Page layout: Kerri Wilson
Editor: Laura Jeanne Gobal   Photo Researcher: Jes Senbergs (management: Debbie Gallagher)
Proofreader: Helena Newton   Illustrator: Robert Shields
                                            Production Controller: Vanessa Johnson

Manufactured in China by Macmillan Production (Asia) Ltd.
Kwun Tong, Kowloon, Hong Kong
Supplier Code: CP January 2010

Acknowledgments

The author and the publisher are grateful to the following for permission to reproduce copyright material:

Front cover photograph of a group of children leaning out of a school bus window, courtesy of Photolibrary/Beau Lark.

Photographs courtesy of © Don Mason/Corbis, 18; © Gabe Palmer/Corbis, 5; © Vicki France/Dreamstime.com, 9; Ira Block/Getty Images, 20; Adam Gault/Getty Images, 17; Tony Lewis/Getty Images, 26; Ed Pritchard/Getty Images, 23; Stockbyte/Getty Images, 19; Paul Thomas/Getty Images, 16; Peter Ziminski/Getty Images, 4; © Hanquan Chen/iStockphoto, 13; © Daumiu/iStockphoto, 21 (top left); © Pavel Losevsky/iStockphoto, 11; © Jane Norton/iStockphoto, 30; © Viorika Prikhodko/iStockphoto, 25; © K. Rus/iStockphoto, 21 (bottom left); © James Steidl/iStockphoto, 12; © Lee Torrens/iStockphoto, 21 (bottom right); © Vasiliki Varvaki/iStockphoto, 21 (top right); Mercedes-Benz Australia/Pacific, 27; Newspix/News Ltd/Glenn Daniels, 29; Photolibrary © Trevor Smith/Alamy, 28; Photolibrary/Inger Helene Boasson, 22; Photolibrary/Mark Henley, 24;© J. Clarke/Shutterstock, 10 (bottom); © Gary 718/Shutterstock, 7; © Joe Gough/Shutterstock, 10 (top right); © Xavier Marchant/Shutterstock, 6; © Vadim Ponomarenko/Shutterstock, 8; © Pino Sub/Shutterstock, 3, 10 (top left).

While every care has been taken to trace and acknowledge copyright, the publisher tenders their apologies for any accidental infringement where copyright has proved untraceable. Where the attempt has been unsuccessful, the publisher welcomes information that would redress the situation.

Contents

When a word is printed in **bold**, you can look up its meaning in the Glossary on page 31.

Living Sustainably

Living sustainably means using things carefully so there is enough left for people in the future. To live sustainably, we need to look after Earth and its **resources**.

If we cut down too many trees now, there will not be enough lumber in the future.

The things we do make a difference. We can use water, energy, and other resources wisely. Our choices can help make a sustainable world.

The choices we make when we travel from one place to another affect Earth.

Using Energy to Get Around

Energy helps people get around. It powers cars, buses, trains, boats, and other vehicles. We use energy to get around all the time.

Boating and waterskiing are fun ways of using energy to get around.

What is Energy?

Energy is power. Power is needed for things to work. Different kinds of energy are needed to do different kinds of work. Heat, light, and electricity are examples of energy.

Electricity powers lights in cities around the world.

Where Does Energy Come From?

The energy we use comes from nature. For example, wood can be burned to create heat or light. **Fossil fuels**, such as coal, oil, and natural gas, can also be burned for energy.

Fossil fuels are found deep underground and can be reached only by digging with expensive machines.

Burning Fossil Fuels

Fossil fuels are a useful source of energy, but burning fossil fuels releases unwanted **greenhouse gases**. These gases are a form of **pollution**. They are harmful to the **environment**.

The gases released by **power plants** can harm the environment.

Renewable and Nonrenewable Energy

Some sources of energy are more sustainable than others. We call these sources renewable energy. Renewable energy does not run out because nature always creates more.

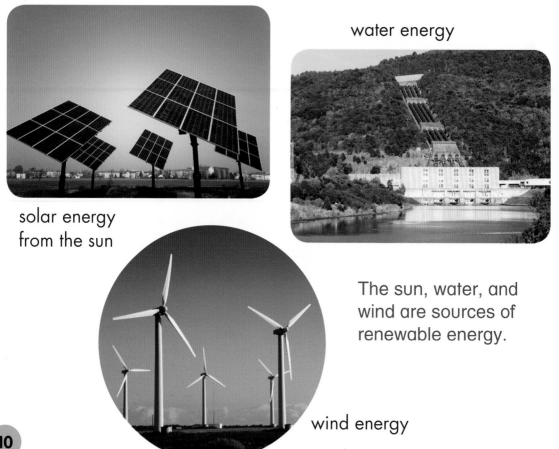

water energy

solar energy from the sun

The sun, water, and wind are sources of renewable energy.

wind energy

Other sources of energy do not last. Once they are used up, nature does not create more. We call these sources nonrenewable energy.

Almost all vehicles today run on gasoline, which is made from a nonrenewable energy source.

Energy from Oil

Oil is a useful form of energy. Fuel is made from oil. It powers cars, trucks, ships, and other vehicles. Fuel makes travel easy. Gasoline and diesel are types of fuel.

Diesel fuel, which is made from oil, is used to power big trucks.

How is Fuel Made from Oil?

Fuel is made from oil at a **refinery**. A refinery takes oil, found deep in the ground, and turns it into gasoline and diesel. These fuels can be used to power engines.

Refineries are large factories where oil is made into fuel.

How Does Fuel Get to the Pump?

Fuel travels a long way to get to the pump. It is found deep in the ground, transported to a refinery and then to a gas station.

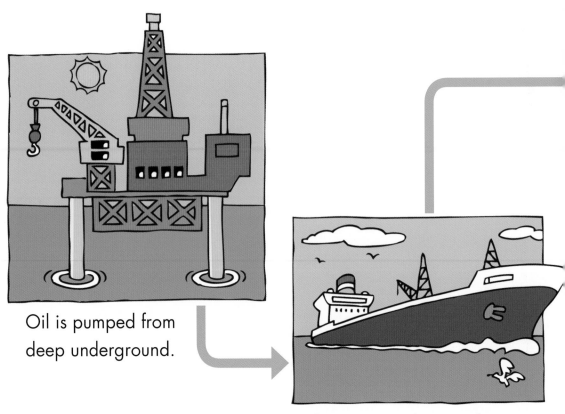

Oil is pumped from deep underground.

Ships carry oil to a refinery.

The refinery turns oil into gasoline or diesel.

Trucks carry gasoline or diesel to a gas station.

At a gas station, pumps fill the tanks in vehicles with gasoline or diesel.

Using Energy Sustainably

If everyone uses energy sustainably, there will always be enough of it. The most important way to use energy sustainably is to save it.

Making the right choices, such as walking instead of driving, helps save energy.

The easiest way to save energy while getting around is to use less fuel. This means we have to use cars less or use them more efficiently.

One way to use cars more efficiently is to share rides with friends.

Save Energy in the Car

A great way to save energy is to make fewer car trips. Going on many short drives uses more energy than one or two well-planned trips.

Getting all of the week's groceries in one trip uses less energy than driving to the store every day.

We can also save energy and fuel by:
- **carpooling** to school, games, and other places our friends might be going to as well
- encouraging our families to take vacations nearby instead of driving farther away
- reminding our parents to check the car's tire pressure

When a car's tires are properly inflated, it uses less fuel.

Save Energy with Public Transportation

Public transportation allows people to get where they need to go by using larger, shared vehicles. Sharing vehicles saves fuel because more people are transported in one vehicle instead of many.

Transporting people by train uses less fuel than when the same people each drive their own cars.

There are many types of public transportation. On land, there are buses, trains, and streetcars. Underground, there are subways, which are underground railroads. On the water, there are ferries.

Ferries, trains, streetcars and buses are types of public transportation.

Save Energy on a Bicycle

Riding a bicycle does not burn any fuel. Bicycles are an **energy-smart** way of getting around. They take less energy to make, use, and repair than cars.

Riding a bicycle is a fun and healthy way to save energy.

For short trips, a bicycle is often the most sustainable choice of transportation. We can ride bicycles for fun or to go to places.

A bicycle uses 53 times less energy than a car.

Save Energy on Foot

Try walking to save fuel. Like riding a bicycle, when we walk somewhere, we do not burn any fuel. Walking is also a good form of exercise.

Walking saves fuel and gives us a chance to stop and look at things.

Walking short distances is an energy-smart choice.

The Two-mile Rule

When deciding whether to walk or use a car to go somewhere, remember the two-mile rule. Walk or cycle if the destination is two miles (3 km) or less away.

Getting Around in the Future

Scientists are working on more sustainable ways to get around. They are testing vehicles that run on sunlight, **hydrogen**, and **alcohol**. They hope to create more fuels from renewable energy sources.

This car is powered by energy from the sun, which is a renewable energy source.

Hybrid Cars

Hybrid cars are powered by a gasoline engine and an electric **generator**. The engine and generator work together to make the car travel much farther on much less fuel.

Hybrid cars use less fuel and release fewer harmful greenhouse gases.

Share the Message

Being energy-smart is an important message to share with your friends. Ask your teacher if your class can make posters about saving fuel to put up around the school.

Share the message about saving fuel with fun posters.

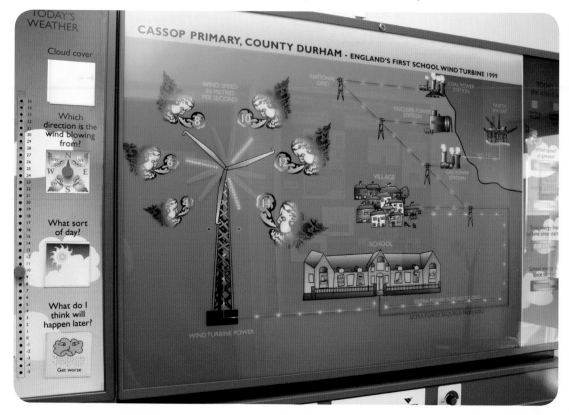

An Energy-smart School

St. Therese's Primary School in Victoria, Australia, encourages students to walk to school with its "walking school bus" program.

Students walk to school with one or more adults instead of taking the bus.

A Sustainable World

Saving energy is one way to live sustainably.
How many ways can you save fuel today?
Your choices and actions will help make a
sustainable world.

Make a list of the things
you can do to save fuel.

Glossary

alcohol   a colorless liquid that can be burned as fuel

carpooling   regularly traveling with a group of people in one car

energy-smart   acting in a way that helps save energy

environment   the air, water, and land that surround us

fossil fuels   the buried remains of plants and animals that form fuels such as oil, coal, and natural gas after millions of years

generator   a machine that creates electrical energy

greenhouse gases   gases found in the air that trap heat around Earth and cause higher temperatures

hydrogen   a gas with no color or smell, that combines with oxygen to form water

pollution   waste that damages the air, water, or land

power plants   factories that produce electricity by burning fossil fuels or by using energy from the sun, wind, or water

refinery   a factory that makes fuels, such as gasoline and diesel, from oil

resources   useful things found on Earth that are hard to replace once they run out

Index